Toast for Mom

Written by Mindy Menschell
Illustrated by Robin Oz

Silver Burdett Ginn
A Division of Simon & Schuster
160 Gould Street
Needham Heights, MA 02194 - 2310

Modern Curriculum Press
A Division of Simon & Schuster
299 Jefferson Road, P.O. Box 480
Parsippany, NJ 07054 - 0480

Design and production by Kirchoff/Wohlberg, Inc.

ISBN: 0-663-59386-7 Silver Burdett Ginn
ISBN: 0-8136-0916-0 Modern Curriculum Press

1 2 3 4 5 6 7 8 9 10 SP 01 00 99 98 97 96 95

When Rose got home, Mom was in
bed. Mom had a bad cold.

"You always take care of me," said
Rose. "So I will take care of you. I will
make you toast."

Rose got the loaf of bread. She
asked her sister Jo to toast the bread.
Then Rose went to talk to Mom.

POP! went the toast.

But Jo was not there. And Rose was
not there. Rose was talking to Mom.

"Mom," said Rose. "Where are my
old green socks?"

"The socks with holes?" asked Mom.

"Yes! The green socks with holes,"
said Rose.

"Those socks are in the ragbag," said
Mom. So Rose went to find the ragbag.

Then Rose smelled the toast. "Hot toast, coming up!" she said. But the toast was cold.

So Rose got the loaf of bread again.
She asked Jo to toast more bread. Then
Rose went to fix up her green sock.

POP! went the toast. But Jo was not
there. And Rose was not there. Rose was
fixing up her old green sock.

She put the sock on her hand. She
put her fingers in the holes. "Those are
the legs," she said.

Then Rose smelled the toast. "Hot toast, coming up!" she said. But the toast was cold.

So Rose got the loaf of bread again.
Jo put more bread in to toast. Then Rose
went to find things for the sock.

POP! went the toast. But Jo was not
there. And Rose was not there. Rose was
fixing up her old green sock.

Rose put a big red dot on the end of the sock. "That's the nose," she said. Then she put on two black dots. "So you can see," she said to the sock.

Rose ran to Mom's bed. "Do you like monsters?" asked Rose.

"Yes!" said Mom. "But I don't want your monster to scare me."

"My monster won't scare you," said Rose. "It will make you smile!"

"I will put on a show for you," said
Rose. "I know this show will cheer you
up. The show has a monster in it."

Rose made the sock monster talk.
She made the sock monster smile.
Then she made the sock monster say,
"The End."

Mom clapped. "I liked your show,"
said Mom. "It made me smile. But Rose
— where is my toast?"

"Oh, Mom, I forgot!" said Rose. "I'll
go get the toast!"

But the toast was cold. And there
was no more bread. "I sure hope Mom
likes cold toast," said Rose.

Rose came back with all the toast.
There was enough toast for Mom, Rose,
Jo, and even a hungry monster.